This book belongs to

Joy of CHRISTMAS

Inspired by Jed

For any correspondence, please visit:
www.sevenflamingtorches.com

JOY OF CHRISTMAS

CATHY NORTEY

Woohoo!

The kids at Nature's Valley School are super duper excited about the holidays!

Counting down the seconds till
the final school bell rings and
the real fun begins!

At the playground, the buzz was all about the gifts under the Christmas tree!

Jonny felt really excited as he
thought about the super cool toy
car that he was going to get soon.

Carla had happy memories that made her smile, like the yummy treats she ate at the Christmas fair.

Sasha's favourite bike, named with lots of love

But wait!

There was one more thing before school ended...

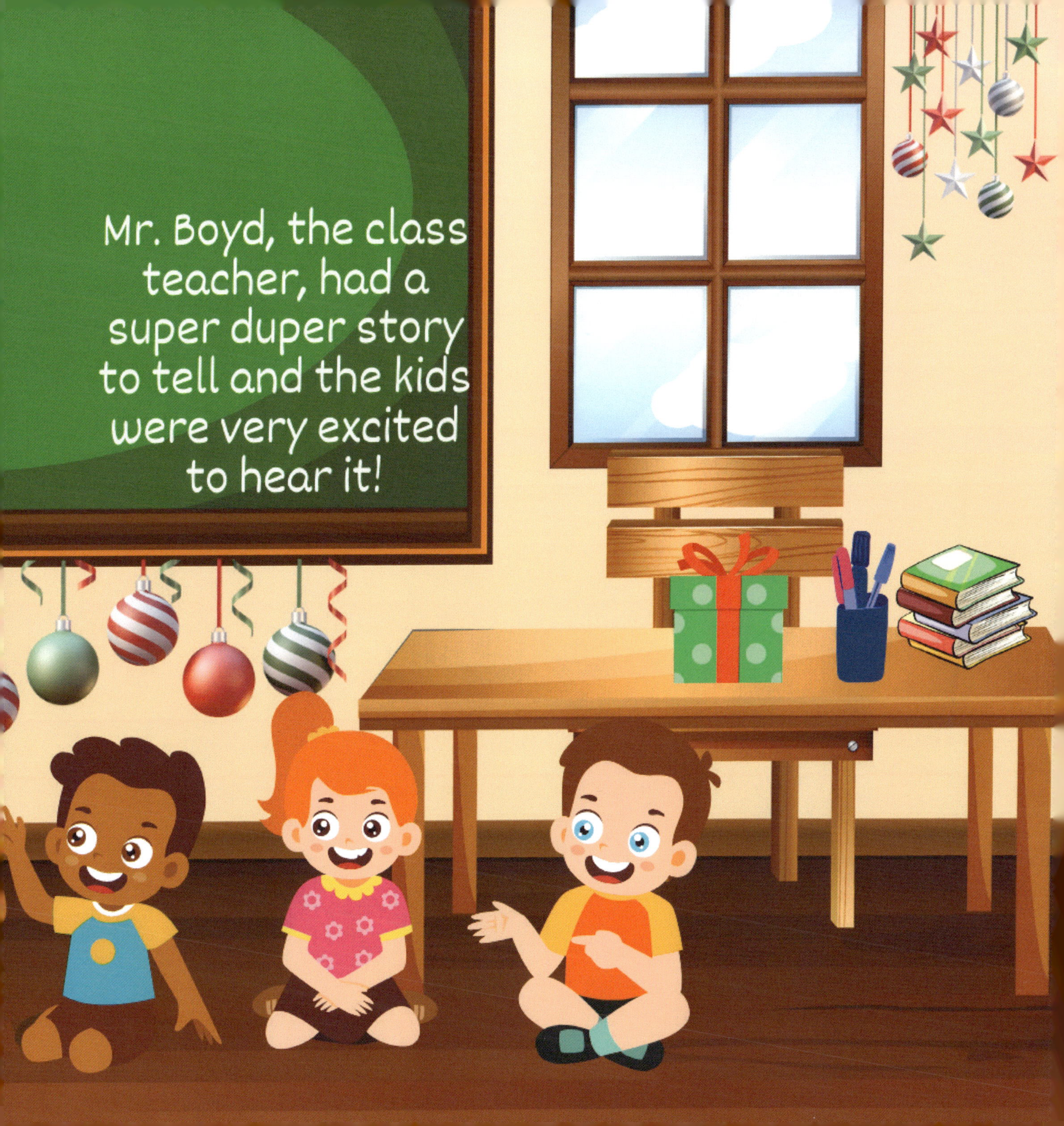

Mr. Boyd, the class teacher, had a super duper story to tell and the kids were very excited to hear it!

A long, long time ago, there was a beautiful garden called Eden. It was so pretty!

It was filled with happy animals who had everything they ever wanted and imagined.

Everything was going well until a sneaky snake told a big lie about a very special tree.

So some sad things
happened and we couldn't
be friends with God
anymore.

As days passed, God did everything to be near to us.

But some people did
things that weren't
very nice.

So, God had a

BIG

plan!

A very special

LAMB

will come to earth to help everyone.

One day, Angel Gabriel visited a young girl in Nazareth and told her some wonderful news!

Guess what?

Mary was going to have a little baby, and God was going to take care of everything.

In the little town of
Bethlehem, it was time for
the baby to be born.

But when Joseph went to find a
place for the baby to be born,
all the rooms were full.

In a simple stable, a cozy manger was given, and guess what?

Little baby
Jesus was
born there!

On this quiet night, all of a sudden heaven opened up and an angel appeared, scaring some shepherds.

The angel announced that a new King was born in a manger.

Lots of pretty angels suddenly appeared in the sky singing...

"Hallelujah in the highest!"

The shepherds found the new baby warmly wrapped in a manger, and they all worshipped him!

Three wise kings followed a star to see the newborn baby. They came with special gifts for the baby!

King Jesus, the Lamb of God,
came into the world...

to make us
all a part of
God's
kingdom.

King Jesus...

...makes wrong things right!

...makes the world a better place!

...shows us God loves us very much!

...takes away all our worries and fears

...helps us every day

...helps sick people get better!

...wants us to be free and joyful

After listening to the beautiful story about baby Jesus, the children were filled with joy.

They started dancing with happiness. Now they know that Christmas is a very special time of the year!

God loves you very much!

He came to earth as a man to show you how much He loves you!

Jesus Christ, God's own Son...

did something very special for you so that you can be super happy and free!

WISHING YOU
a Merry
Christmas
and a
WONDERFUL
New Year

Printed in Great Britain
by Amazon

33686493R00023